THE BONE WARS

The True Story of an Epic Battle to Find Dinosaur Fossils

written by
Jane Kurtz

illustrated by
Alexander Vidal

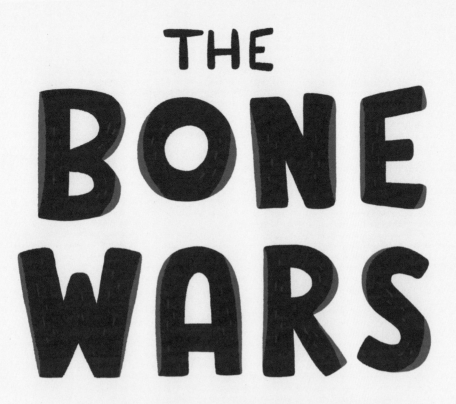

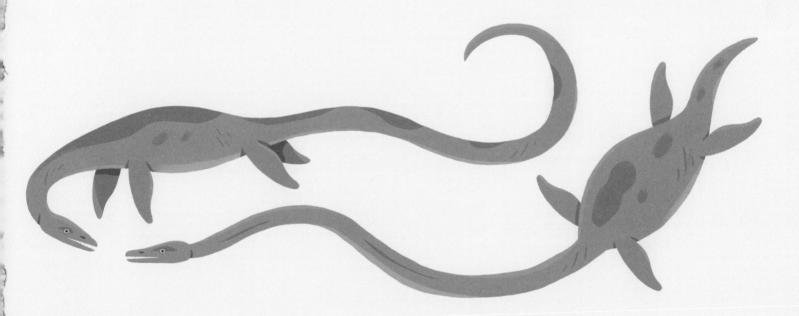

Beach Lane Books
New York   London   Toronto   Sydney   New Delhi

You stand in a museum, captivated
by a dinosaur skeleton.

Amazing!
Incredible!

You might not know that behind that skeleton,
all neatly fit together, is something as mean
and messy as . . .

the Bone Wars.

In 1863 two smart, bold young men met for the first time. They had a lot in common.

O. C. Marsh and Edward Drinker Cope
were fascinated by science.

O.C. MARSH

O. C. did not like his first name (Othniel), so he used his initials. He puffed with pride because he graduated from Yale University, which had the best science program in America.

EDWARD COPE

Edward left school when he was sixteen. But he continued to teach himself, with a lot of help from a scientist who had recognized and named the very first dinosaur skeleton found in America. Edward was curious, a quick learner, and a lively writer.

Edward Cope and O. C. Marsh. Friends forever.

Cope and Marsh wrote letters to each
other. They spent a cold and rainy
week tromping around fossil beds
in New Jersey.

Cope named an amphibian
fossil after Marsh.

Ptyonius marshii

Marsh named a serpent
fossil after Cope.

Mosasaurus copeanus

Yes, friends forever.

Until...

Cope received a jumble of fossilized bones that arrived in wooden crates. He slowly puzzled out that the bones must belong to a prehistoric marine reptile no one had ever imagined—35 feet long, with fins and a long, snaky tail.

He wrote a scientific paper describing the fascinating animal: Elasmosaurus.

Wow, was he proud!

Marsh walked in and admired his friend's hard work.

Until...

he spotted something interesting.

Interesting and ...wrong.

Cope had attached the
Elasmosaurus skull to its tail.

Cope's
Elasmosaurus

Correct
Elasmosaurus

Hoo boy! Marsh was delighted to point out his friend's mistake.

Cope hastily tried to buy and destroy every
copy of the paper he had written.

He was embarrassed.

He was angry.

And that's when...

the Bone Wars began.

From now on, it would be an all-out competition to make the next big discovery.

Marsh found a wing finger of a pterodactyl— a creature he declared must have looked like a gigantic flying dragon.

Cope found a bone of a huge mosasaur that swam through the sea.

More, more, more exciting bones piled up.

Giant turtles.

Birds with teeth.

Until...

one day two hikers spotted giant dinosaur bones poking
out of the ground in Colorado.

No one had ever seen huge bones like these before! When Cope and
Marsh found out about the amazing discovery, they both wanted
to get their hands on all the fossils, puzzle out the skeletons of
these mighty lizards, and make up a name for each new creature.

What could be more exciting?

The race was on!
Cope and Marsh each sent teams west
to explore and dig.

Who could find the
BIGGEST, BEST
new dinosaurs?

Soon, train cars full of bones
chugged east so Cope and Marsh
could study them and put them
together like puzzle pieces.

The world was waiting eagerly to read
about these fascinating creatures.

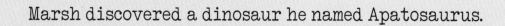

Marsh discovered a dinosaur he named Apatosaurus.

Then Cope found the biggest
dinosaur anyone had ever seen.
He named it Camarasaurus.

Both teams tried to keep their finds secret.
Code names? Why not! Disguises? Yes! Snooping
and trickery? Of course!

One of Marsh's workers was sent to spy on someone who used to be Marsh's friend but had switched sides.

Cope tried charm. He showed up at a Marsh dig and sang a funny song with a refrain that sounded like a coyote's howl.

Marsh's men liked him—
but they didn't trust him.

Cope's and Marsh's teams played dirty.

Marsh's workers left a skull and some teeth from two different animals in a spot that would make Cope think they belonged together. (The mistake wasn't discovered for twenty years.)

Workers from both sides occasionally blew up smaller bones they didn't need so the other team wouldn't get them.

They filled excavation pits with dirt and stones to keep the other team from making good finds.

Cope's and Marsh's teams even tossed rocks at each other!

As the bones piled up, Cope and Marsh described and named new dinosaurs as fast as they could.

Because they were in a hurry to win, mistakes also piled up.

Each man had some bones from a spiked dinosaur that Marsh assumed stood on its hind legs. Cope named it Hypsirhophus. But Marsh beat him to it—with the name Stegosaurus.

Marsh named Morosaurus only to find Cope had previously named it Camarasaurus.

Marsh even named the same dinosaur twice—first Apatosaurus, then Brontosaurus. Since the name Apatosaurus came first, the name Brontosaurus had to go.

For years Cope and Marsh studied their bones and wrote papers and criticized each other. Their friends and other scientists felt squeezed by all the squabbles.

Then in 1890 the *New York Herald* published an article with the headline:

SCIENTISTS WAGE BITTER WARFARE

Hoo boy.

Enemies forever and now everyone knew it.

Until...

the rivalry ruined both Cope and Marsh.

They each ended up disgraced and broke.

Marsh never had a family. His students sometimes called
him the Great Dismal Swamp (behind his back, of course).

At one point Cope had more bones than he could fit in his house. His wife, some people said, found one too many snakes in her shoe and left. So now he lived alone too, except for a giant tortoise and a Gila monster.

When Cope died he donated his brain to science, hoping it would prove to be bigger than Marsh's brain.

In the end the Bone Wars destroyed both smart, determined, bold men. So nobody really won the Bone Wars.

Except...

thanks to Marsh and Cope, America eventually got museums full of dinosaur bones. The whole world was captivated by dinosaurs.

So, if you've ever stared up at a dinosaur skeleton at a museum and imagined a whole amazing ancient world...

congratulations!

You won the Bone Wars!

Author's Note

Marsh discovered approximately eighty new dinosaur species.

Cope discovered only fifty-six new species, but he published a record number of papers and trained younger paleontologists—like Henry Osborn, who displayed the first *T. rex* skeleton.

Cope's brain is still at a research institute in Philadelphia. (Marsh did not take the bait, and his skull was buried along with his body when he died. So we'll never know who had the bigger brain!)

Marsh's rush to use the name Brontosaurus *still* causes confusion. Most paleontologists stopped using that name more than a hundred years ago. Gradually, other dinosaur lovers dropped it too. Now a recent study argues that Brontosaurus and Apatosaurus are separate species. The debate continues!

Many more details about the days of the big dinosaur discoveries are out there for you to read. In fact, thousands of people over many decades have read about, studied, and even played a card game about the Bone Wars. Some think it actually began before Cope's Elasmosaurus mistake. They say the bad feelings started when Marsh visited the New Jersey fossil beds with Cope and paid workers to send him anything interesting that they uncovered.

While Cope and Marsh were piling up bones and trying to get the best of each other, their major discoveries were brought to public attention through newspapers and magazines. After their deaths, the skeletons they had put together inspired murals and museum exhibits that people found fascinating. A new generation of scientists rushed to find even more skeletons—which led to a huge interest in dinosaurs. Since then, paleontologists all over the world have gone on to find many more dinosaur bones, as well as dinosaur eggs, skin, footprints, and fossilized poop.

And plenty of smart, determined scientists are figuring out more, more, more.

Illustrator's Note

Many of the illustrated creatures in this book will likely look quite outdated to a modern audience. To immerse readers in the prehistoric world as it was envisioned by O. C. Marsh and Edward Cope, I drew inspiration from the paleoart of the 1800s. Marsh and Cope were working only a few decades after the term "dinosaur" even came into use, and illustrations from that era often depicted prehistoric creatures as strange and monstrous, just a few steps removed from dragons.

I also wanted my illustrations to show how our understanding of these creatures has changed over time. I became interested in dinosaurs as a child in the 1980s, and I remember imagining them as scaly, slow-moving reptiles. In the decades since, it's been incredible watching this image evolve as new discoveries are made—that they were likely warm-blooded, that some were agile hunters or caring parents, and that some were even covered in feathers. As much as we've learned, our understanding of these creatures is incomplete and ever evolving. Who knows what fossils will be discovered in the future or what groundbreaking new theories will be developed—perhaps even by someone reading this book.

Special thanks to David W. Krause,
senior curator of vertebrate paleontology at
the Denver Museum of Nature & Science,
for reviewing this book.

Selected Sources

Conniff, Richard. *House of Lost Worlds: Dinosaurs, Dynasties, and the Story of Life on Earth.* New Haven, CT: Yale University Press, 2016.

Davidson, Jane Pierce. *The Bone Sharp: The Life of Edward Drinker Cope.* Philadelphia: The Academy of Natural Sciences of Philadelphia, 1997.

Davis, Mark, and Anna Saraceno, producers. "Dinosaur Wars." PBS: American Experience. Aired January 17, 2011. Accessed 2022. https://www.pbs.org/wgbh/americanexperience/films/dinosaur/.

Jaffe, Mark. *The Gilded Dinosaur: The Fossil War Between E. D. Cope and O. C. Marsh and the Rise of American Science.* New York: Three Rivers Press, 2000.

Randall, David K. *The Monster's Bones: The Discovery of T. Rex and How It Shook Our World.* New York: W. W. Norton, 2022.

Sullivan, Robert, and Spencer Lucas. "Edward Drinker Cope, Pennsylvania's Greatest Naturalist." *Pennsylvania Heritage.* Fall 2005.

Switek, Brian. *The Secret Life of Bones: Their Origins, Evolution and Fate.* Richmond, UK: Duckworth Books, 2019.

Suggested Reading

Colson, Rob. *Dinosaur Bones: And What They Tell Us.* London: Firefly Books, 2016.

Dee, Nicky. *The Bone Wars: Clash of the Dinosaur Hunters!* London: Dragonfly Group Ltd., 2017.

Hall, Ashley. *Fossils for Kids: A Junior Scientist's Guide to Dinosaur Bones, Ancient Animals, and Prehistoric Life on Earth.* Emeryville, CA: Rockridge Press, 2020.

Kerley, Barbara. *The Dinosaurs of Waterhouse Hawkins.* New York: Scholastic Press, 2001.

McNamara, Margaret. *The Dinosaur Expert.* New York: Penguin Random House, 2018.

Skeers, Linda. *Dinosaur Lady: The Daring Discoveries of Mary Anning, the First Paleontologist.* Naperville, IL: Sourcebooks, 2020.

Waters, Kate. *Curious about Fossils.* New York: Penguin Random House, 2016.

For David, Jonathan, Rebekah, Ellemae, and Noh,
who rattled off complicated names, put together puzzles,
and generally loved dinosaurs with me—J. K.

For my parents, who never refused a request to visit
the natural history museum—A. V.

BEACH LANE BOOKS • An imprint of Simon & Schuster Children's Publishing Division • 1230 Avenue of the Americas, New York, New York 10020 • Text © 2023 by Jane Kurtz • Illustration © 2023 by Alexander Vidal • Book design by Lauren Rille © 2023 by Simon & Schuster, Inc. • All rights reserved, including the right of reproduction in whole or in part in any form. • BEACH LANE BOOKS and colophon are trademarks of Simon & Schuster, Inc. • For information about special discounts for bulk purchases, please contact Simon & Schuster Special Sales at 1-866-506-1949 or business@simonandschuster.com. • The Simon & Schuster Speakers Bureau can bring authors to your live event. For more information or to book an event, contact the Simon & Schuster Speakers Bureau at 1-866-248-3049 or visit our website at www.simonspeakers.com. • The text for this book was set in Bulletin. • The illustrations for this book were rendered digitally. • Manufactured in China • 0723 SCP • First Edition • 2 4 6 8 10 9 7 5 3 1 • Library of Congress Cataloging-in-Publication Data • Names: Kurtz, Jane, author. | Vidal, Alexander, illustrator. • Title: The bone wars : the true story of an epic battle to find dinosaur fossils / Jane Kurtz ; Illustrated by Alexander Vidal. • Description: First edition. | New York, New York : Beach Lane Books, an imprint of Simon & Schuster Children's Publishing Division, [2023] | Includes bibliographical references. | Audience: Ages 4–8 | Audience: Grades 2–3 | Summary: "Discover the true story of the race between two paleontologists, O. C. Marsh and Edward Cope, to find dinosaur fossils in this nonfiction picture book."– Provided by publisher. • Identifiers: LCCN 2022046884 (print) | LCCN 2022046885 (ebook) | ISBN 9781534493643 (hardcover) | ISBN 9781534493650 (ebook) • Subjects: LCSH: Cope, E. D. (Edward Drinker), 1840–1897–Juvenile literature. | Marsh, Othniel Charles, 1831–1899–Juvenile literature. | Paleontologists–United States–Biography–Juvenile literature. | Paleontology–United States–History–19th century–Juvenile literature. | Fossils–Collection and preservation–United States–History–19th century–Juvenile literature. • Classification: LCC QE707.C63 K87 2023 (print) | LCC QE707.C63 (ebook) | DDC 560.92/273–dc23/eng20230119 • LC record available at https://lccn.loc.gov/2022046884 • LC ebook record available at https://lccn.loc.gov/2022046885